A Rat R

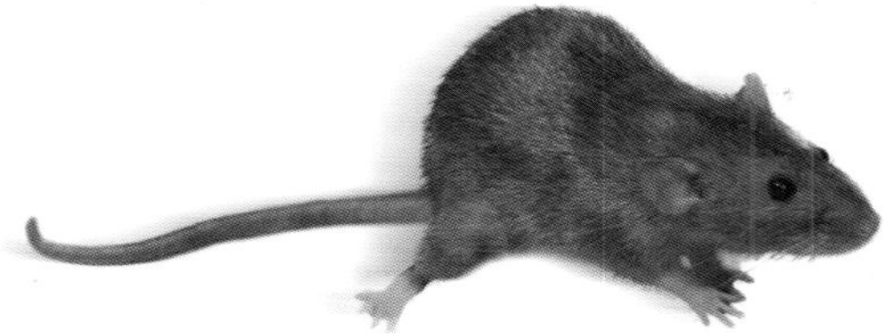

4 ckeur

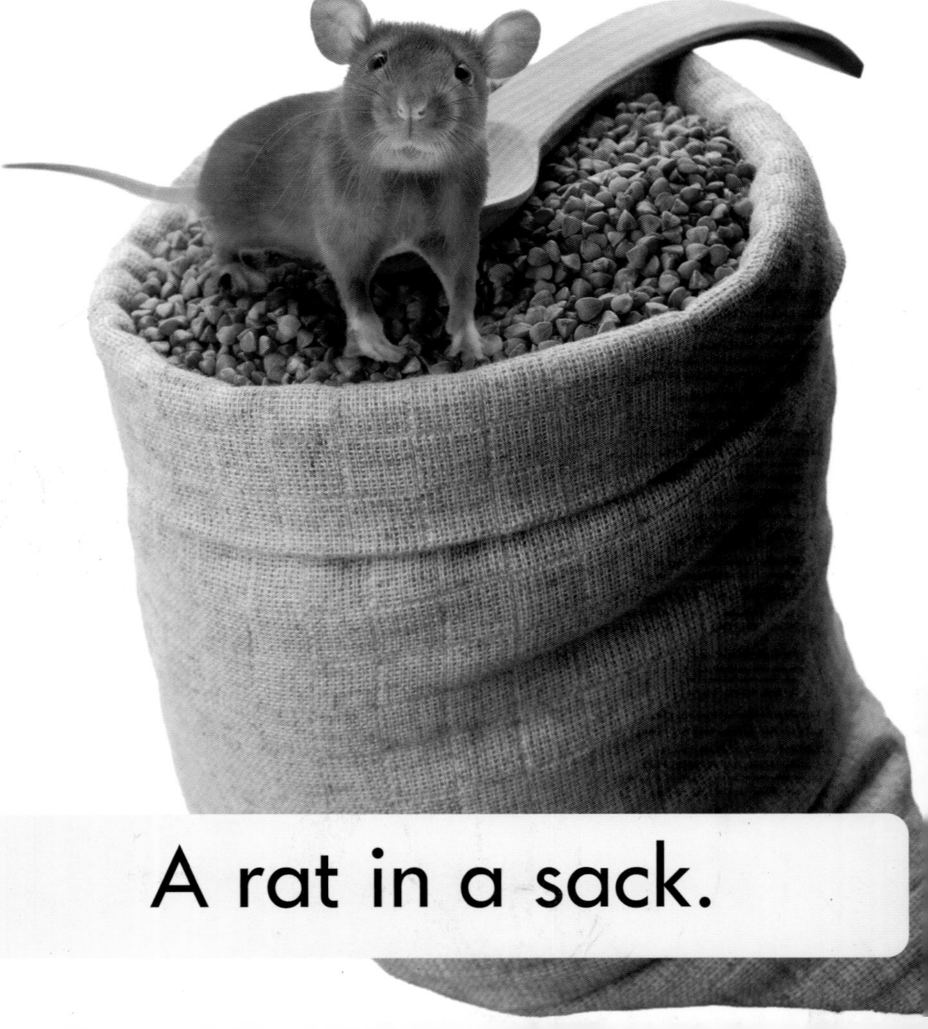

A rat in a sack.

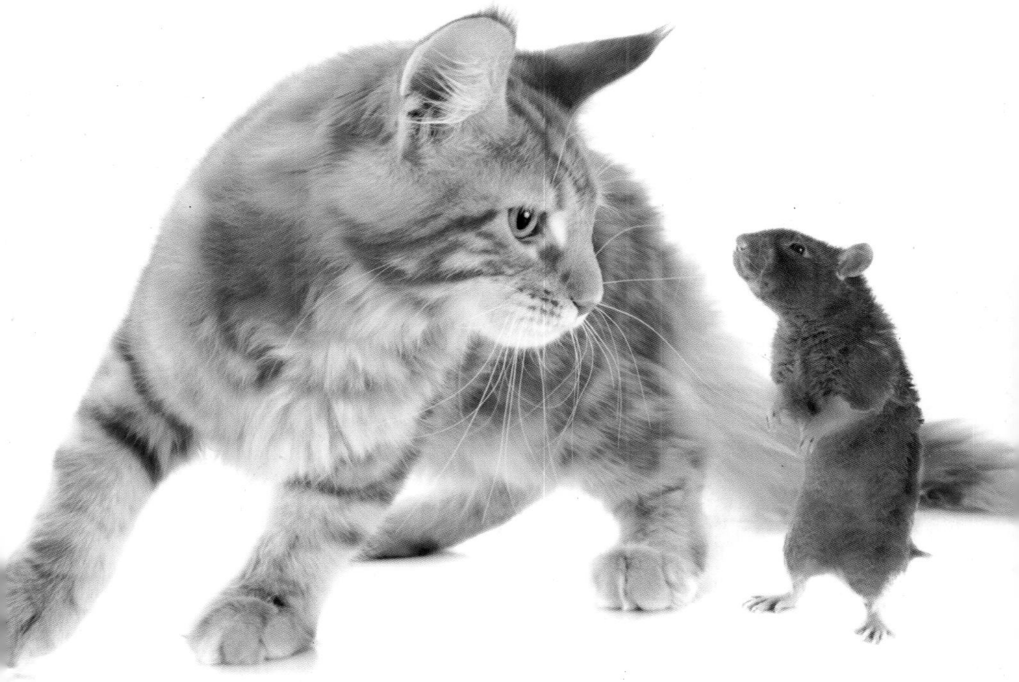

A cat picks at rat.

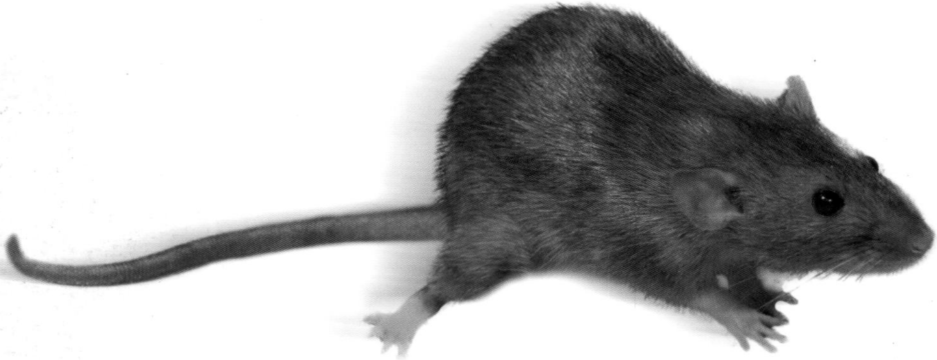

The rat runs!

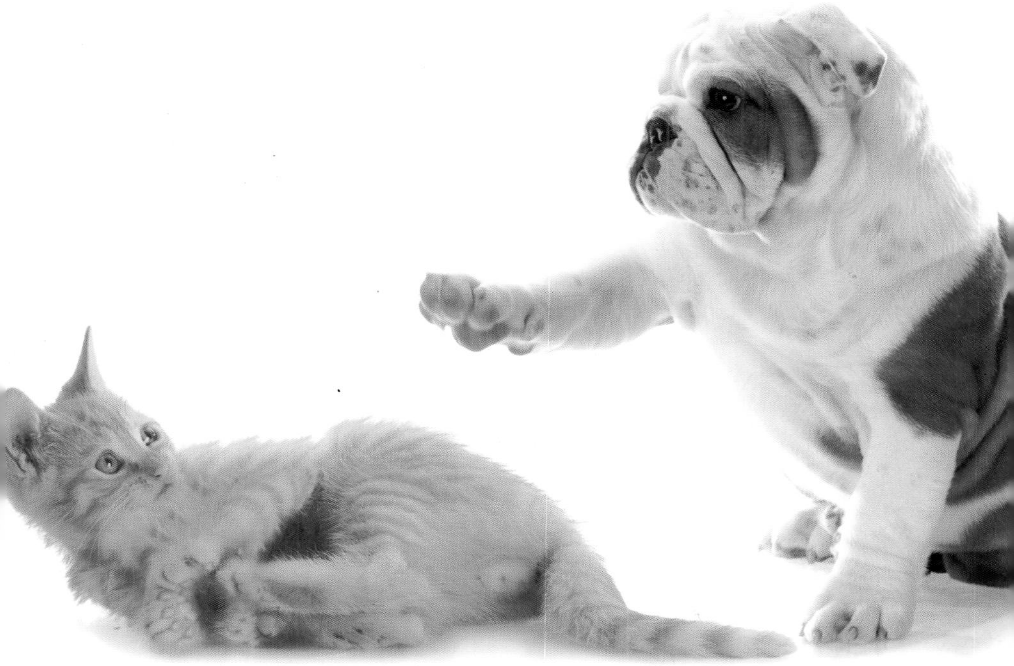

A dog kicks a cat.

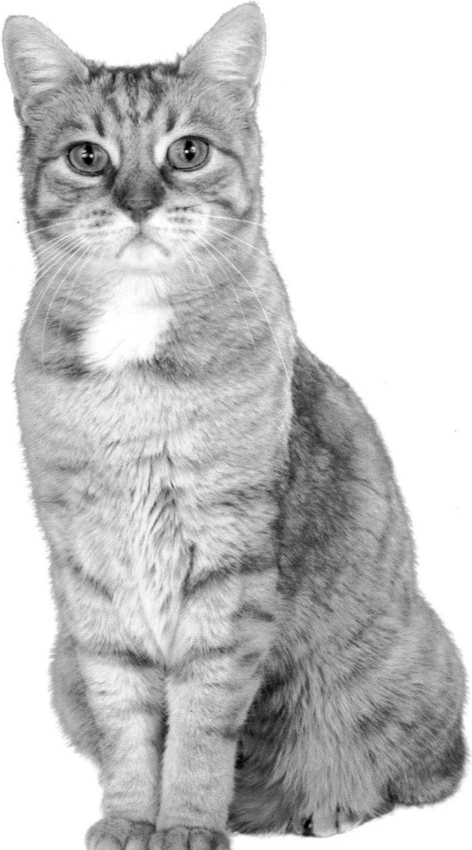

Cat gets sad.

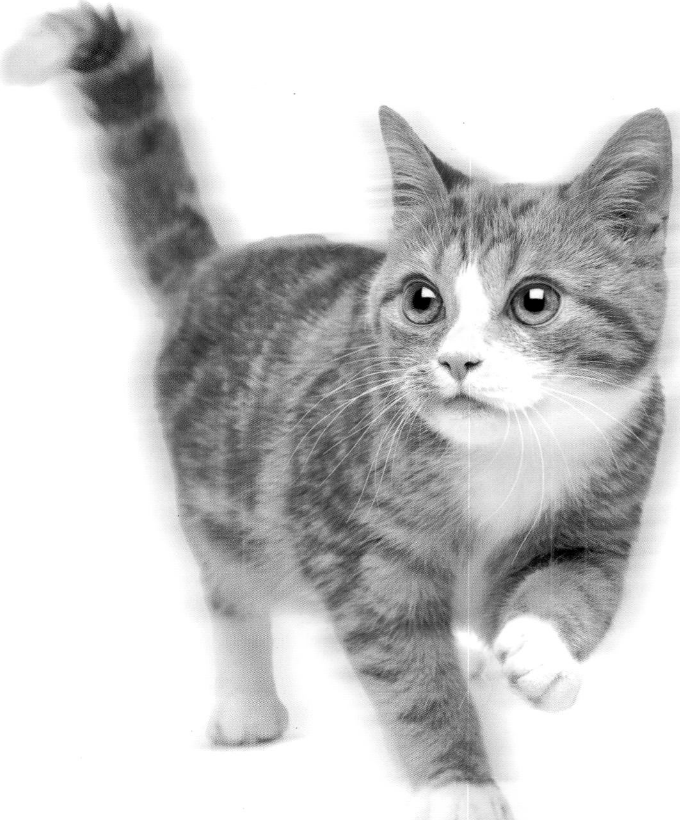

The cat runs!

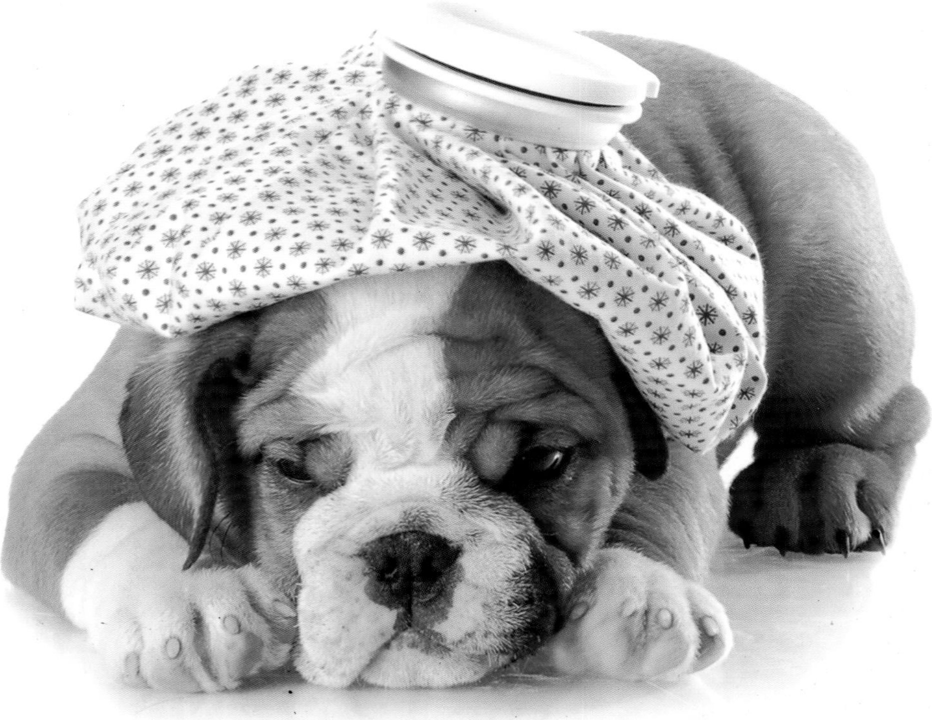

Dog gets sick.